RESCUED

Rescue Mission for the Kingdom

JAMIE WILLIAMS

Rescued: Rescue Mission for the Kingdom

© 2023 by Jamie Williams

Unless otherwise noted, all scriptural quotations are taken from the *New King James Version*®. Copyright © 1982 by Thomas Nelson. Used by permission. All rights reserved.

Scripture quotations marked (NIV) are taken from the Holy Bible, NEW INTERNATIONAL VERSION®, NIV® Copyright © 1973, 1978, 1984, 2011 by Biblica, Inc.® Used by permission. All rights reserved worldwide.

ISBNs: 979-8-9877024-0-6 (Paperback)

979-8-9877024-1-3 (Ebook)

Printed in the United States of America.

Acknowledgments

This book took a lot for me to write, and I'm so happy that it has finally come to pass.

This book wouldn't be possible without my dad, a god-fearing man and my best friend whom I lost when I was ten years old. He encouraged my love for music and he showed me that without hard work it isn't possible to give it your all, even when you are tired, and to keep persevering to do everything with God and His grace! Thank you, Dad, for showing me it is possible.

I also wouldn't have been able to do it without my grandfather, who took me, my mom, and my baby brother into his house five years ago when we were so broken. Without him and God, we wouldn't have been put back together. He took on the role of a father in my life and is the kindest man I know. I would not be standing where I am today without his guidance and fatherly love, and he showed me how to love the Lord. thank you, Grandad, for showing me true kindness!

I also want to thank a mighty woman of valor, a mighty woman of God; thank you, Elsie, for praying for me and teaching me about the Word more than anyone else. You blow my mind! Thank you for telling me, "You are enough." Thank you for showing me what true obedience looks like.

I wouldn't be able to do this without Nancy Watson, a woman who brought me laughter and encouraged me to turn to God first. You are one of the strongest people I know. Thank you, Nancy, for being the Naomi to my mom. Thank you for being a part of my life. I love you, Nancy, and I don't know where my family would be without you!

Finally, thank you to my mom for being there for me. Thank you for being the strongest person I know and for showing me the ways of the Word. Thank you for being you! I was in such deep brokenness, and without you, I'd still be in darkness. God truly took my shattered life and turned it into blessing.

When I felt alone, I had an army of people backing me up and praying for me. Thank you, God, for putting each of these people in my life. I'll never stop thanking you, God, for my rescue story.

Contents

Foreword

> Let no one despise you for your youth,
> but set the believers an example in
> speech, in conduct, in love, in faith, in
> purity. (1 Timothy 4:12)

In this verse, Paul talks about being a young servant of the Lord, and we are so proud to see Jamie stepping out and becoming just that.

A few years ago, Jamie came to our church and gave a word about depression. She spoke directly from her heart, and we were so blessed by her willingness to share her testimony about how the Lord helped her overcome that struggle. The Bible says that we are overcomers by the blood of the Lamb and the word of our testimony. There is power in sharing the struggles the Lord has brought us through.

We cannot wait to read this book, and we are so proud of you, Jamie, for stepping out in faith and writing it!

— Mary and Henry Turner
Youth Leaders, Anchor Outreach

Introduction

***M**y beloved generation,*
YOU are the reason I wrote this book. Yes, I am talking to you, the one reading this right now and holding this page. You see, when we go through struggles in this life (and trust me, you will have struggles), there is a huge benefit that waits on the other side. Now you hold a life preserver to be used to pull out another precious life. That preserver may get them through the next twenty-four hours, then the next year, until eventually they will be on that shore, throwing that life preserver back out to the next person who feels like they are drowning. God wastes nothing.

I have observed that when the situation looks hopeless, that is when He does His finest work. Looking around, I see that my generation is being defined by the world—and I have had enough. No more! I believe my generation will take the kingdom further then it has gone in the past. We will be the next Jesus Revolution.

I do not care what the world says, what the results are, or even what your mommy and daddy said. God calls us to live—not just coast by floating there forever—but living the abundant life He went to the cross for you to grab hold of. It is true that in this life you will have trouble, but take heart, Jesus has overcome the world, and when you partner with Christ, you will too.

> But now, do not therefore be grieved or angry with yourselves because you sold me here; for God sent me before you to preserve life. (Genesis 45:5)

Part 1: Lessons from Life

Rescue Mission

It's time to start rescuing for the kingdom. We are all anointed; set apart. It's time to start throwing lifesavers out—it's your time!

> He has delivered us from the power of darkness and conveyed us into the kingdom of the Son of His love, in whom we have redemption through His blood, the forgiveness of sins. (Colossians 1:13-14)

We are rescued; we are saved. Whatever we may face, let Him shine through it. Let Him take care of it. The God I serve knows only how to triumph! You are enough. You are chosen. You are anointed and appointed for such a time as this.

> The thief does not come except to steal, and to kill, and to destroy. I have come that they may have life, and that they may have it more abundantly. (John 10:10)

The enemy only comes for harm, but my God, the living God, comes to heal. The battle belongs to Him!

this isn't just a rescue story, but a rescue mission—and it's time for you to start your mission. It's your time to step up. I pray a boldness over you. I pray you will have joy to start sharing your testimony, start writing your books, and to start sharing His Word. This is the next generation. Your time is NOW!

> I can do all things through Christ who strengthens me. (Philippians 4:13)

You can do all things—nothing is impossible with Him! Don't let the enemy discourage you; he's always going to tell you that you can't do things for God. Don't let him hold you back from what God has created you for. Let his discouragement become strength and show the enemy what you are made of and what God has made you for.

You are anointed and appointed to do mighty things, now start doing them!

Life Preserver

When you feel like you are drowning in the water, God is there. Just pray that He will throw out the life preserver into the deep waters and bring you out of it.

> Then Peter got down out of the boat, walked on the water and came toward Jesus. But when he saw the wind, he was afraid and, beginning to sink, cried out, "Lord, save me!" Immediately Jesus reached out his hand and caught him. "You of little faith," he said, "why did you doubt?" (Matthew 14:30-31 NIV)

Even though Peter had little faith, God never hesitated to save him. He immediately reached down and pulled Peter out of the water.

> If you have the faith as small as a mustard seed…nothing will be impossible for you. (Matthew 17:20)

Even when you are drowning in sin, depression, pain, bitterness, and hate, God will not hesitate to reach

His hand into those deep waters and He will pull out of it. Just call on Him because He has called you to be set apart.

> When you pass though deep waters, I will be with you; and when you pass through the rivers, they will not sweep over you. When you walk through the fire, you will not be burned; the flames will not set you ablaze. (Isaiah 43:2 NIV)

For my God, the living God who brought me out of my depression, my pain, my mourning, and my deep waters, will do the same for you. The next time you are at a pool, step into the water and notice how you immediately will sink to the bottom. So even when Peter began to sink, Jesus never let him fall. He was on the other side of the lake, and the disciples couldn't recognize who He was, so Peter called out to Jesus.

> Shortly before dawn Jesus went out to them, walking on the lake. When the disciples saw him walking on the lake, they were terrified. "It's a ghost," they said, and cried out in fear. But Jesus immediately said to them: "Take courage! It is I. Don't be afraid." "Lord, if it's you," Peter replied, "tell me to come to you on the water." (Matthew 14:25-28 NIV)

When Peter began to sink, the Lord instantly came across the lake and saved Peter. No matter how far you think you are from God, He will be there instantly if you call on Him. Be with you through it all and will never leave or forsake you!

When Jesus said, "Come," Peter was the only one with enough courage and faith to step out of the boat. Peter didn't walk out on the water alone—he walked on the word Jesus said: come. Your promises are not forgotten; walk on your promises. Walk on His words.

Walk in the deep water even when you think you can't. Even when you think you're too far gone. Even when you doubt He is there. He will pull you out of the pain, the depression, the anxiety, and the misery and walk with you through whatever situation you are in.

Guard Your Heart

The Bible tells us to guard our hearts with the breastplate of righteousness. How does one guard their heart? Through the power of intersession. One of my favorite books is by Nora Emge, who has been a long-time spiritual mentor to me and my mom. Her book, *The Power of Intercession,* saved our lives and taught us the power of intersession.

In the book she talks about when she was a young girl and that she prayed until there was breakthrough for her family. She also tells how she uses the power of intersession to this day and has slayed so many giants in her life!

You must pray until you see change.

The power of intersession can move mountains and change lives. Take your battles to your prayer closet and you will defeat some of the biggest giants in your life.

You won't see change until you put it at the foot of the Father. The world will always fail you, but the Word will always triumph.

Don't just pray for yourself, but pray for your family, your friends—even your enemies—until you see change. The attacks of the enemy are the same. What he said to me, he will say to you. That's why you must be prepared and have a guarded heart so you don't fall into sin with his schemes. He will tell you that you're not enough, you're a failure and a disappointment, and that you're unqualified. Well, God doesn't call the qualified, He qualifies the called.

Trust me, I am in no way qualified to write a book at all. I'm a fifteen-year-old girl who learns something new every day. But God has qualified me. He called me to write this book and He gives me the wisdom to write these things. It's not me—it's straight from the Holy Spirit.

Not everyone will understand your calling, and that's okay because your calling is not a conference call!

If you are battling generational curses, strongholds, and grief, and the enemy is lying to you and saying you won't get through this, well, I'm living proof that you will. My mom is living proof that you will. My six-year-old brother is living proof that you will!

My mom lost her sister and her two brothers, who were her best friends. She also lost her mother, her husband, and many other things that life threw at her, but through faith and God's Word she got through it all. When my dad passed away, my mother, my two-year-old brother, and I all fell into a depression—I suffered the most. We were all in mourning, and the enemy would tell me lies such as, "You're not enough, you're a disappointment to your family—and not just your family, but to God; you'll fail Him too." The enemy would say, "You're God's worst failure." Then he would tell me that I had nothing to live for. He would taunt me in nightmares.

Then one day everything changed. I had a "but God" moment. The Lord gave me a dream. In the dream I was trying to kill myself, but before I did, I said, "God, what do I have to live for?" And my three-year-old little brother, who didn't know left from right, let alone anything about suicide, said, "You have me to live for." What I didn't know is that so many people, including my mother, family, friends, cousins, aunts, and uncles were all in their prayer closets praying for me to live!

I jumped out of my bed with tears rolling down my face. A couple days later, my mom gave her testimony. A day later, my little brother gave his testimony AT FOUR YEARS OLD! He not only gave his life to the Lord at that young age, but he defeated a generational curse! Then the last of the three, I gave my testimony too. The Lord took me from my despair and placed me into my destiny! It's been a rollercoaster ever since!

As I grew closer to God I started applying the full armor of God and defeated generational curses I didn't know I had; I began to break out of strongholds with spiritual "sledgehammers" of prayer. God came with spiritual bolt cutters, cutting me out of the chains one by one. The Lord has changed my life and transformed it!

You must guard your heart and denounce the lies of the enemy as they come to you, and fight your battles through intersession. You will see change, I promise you.

Lean On That Faith

The children of Israel were struck with the spirit of fear. They wanted to go back to Egypt.

> Is this not the word that we told you in Egypt, saying, "Let us alone that we may serve the Egyptians"? For it would have been better for us to serve the Egyptians than that we should die in the wilderness. (Exodus 14:12)

Just because it's what you are used to, doesn't mean it's what God has for you. It's time to move out of that slave mindset, that "comfort zone," and move into the Promised Land.

> But Moses said to the people, "Fear not! Stand firm! And see the salvation of the Lord, which He will show you today. (Exodus 14:13, *my paraphrase*)

We need to put on the mindset of salvation! The most important thing is that you arm your mind against the attacks of the enemy. He will try pushing you back into that slave mindset, making you think the old way is the only way.

No circumstance is greater then my God! Guard yourself with the helmet of salvation. Ephesians 6:12 tells us that our fight is not against flesh and blood, but against principalities, against powers, against the rulers of the darkness of this world, and against spiritual forces of evil in heavenly places.

Your time alone in prayer is your transformation time. You will not see transformation unless you pray for transformation. Your situation won't just change, but *you* will change! You will be a new person in Christ.

Here are a few promises from the Word about how God will help us fight our battles:

> The Lord will fight for you, and you shall hold your peace. (Exodus 14:14)

Give the Lord your battles and hold your peace!

> Be still, and know that I am God; I will be exalted among the nations, I will be exalted in the earth! (Psalm 46:10)

Take your battles to your prayer closet, not to the world. Give it to God instead of dealing with it in a fleshly way and starting an argument. Take it to God, for He will fight for you!

Then Moses stretched out his hand over the sea; and the Lord caused the sea to go back by a strong east wind all that night, and made the sea into dry land, and the waters were divided. So the children of Israel went into the midst of the sea on the dry ground, and the waters were a wall to them on their right hand and on their left. (Exodus 14:21-22)

If there's a sea in front of you and you feel hopeless, I have good news for you! The same God who parted the water for Moses is the same God we have now. God will send that east wind into your life and the water will part into a highway for you to walk on leave the old and walk into the promise. Just have faith and watch where it can take you! A little bit of faith can lead you into your promise.

There's nothing that my God, the living God, can't do!

Stomp

The serpent deceived me. (Genesis 3:13)

A serpent can not only refer to a creature, but also to someone who is sly or dangerous and can exploit someone's trust in them to betray that person.

Most people don't realize that snakes, or serpents, don't have ears, which makes them deaf. It doesn't matter what kind of noise you make to scare the snake away, it won't hear you. It's actually *vibrations* that frighten the serpent.

The serpent is afraid of your stomp, so keep marching on—shake the room! As you walk and frighten the snake, it flees.

Matthew 10:16 tells us to be as wise as a serpent and gentle as a dove. Serpents have great wisdom, but you can't be gentle when defeating a serpent. Be aware that it can shed its skin. Watch out because no matter how many times it sheds it's skin, it is still a snake. Be aware of that before letting them back into your life. There's a difference between forgiveness and letting someone back in. You can forgive and forget, but some people aren't meant to be there in the first place.

> And I will put enmity between you and
> the woman, and between your offspring
> and hers; he will crush your head, and you
> will strike his heel. (Genesis 3:15 NIV)

Keep stomping! The snake fears it because it knows the power of your stomp. God has anointed you to slay snakes. You are not fighting to *get* the victory, but you are fighting *from a place* of victory, for Jesus Christ has already defeated satan!

The enemy is a liar, but he can only harm you if you choose to believe his lies and are deceived by him! A snake is meant to move on his belly—not to have a seat at your table; remember that!

If you have a serpent crawling around in your life, read Ephesians 6:15 and "shod your feet with the preparation of the gospel of peace." Put your boots on and start stomping and dancing like David through your situation until your heel crushes the head of the serpent and you have peace!

Graves to Grace

Put down your shovels and pick up your swords. It's time to stop digging your own grave but fight for grace. Shut your ears to the lies of the world and start listening to the Word of God, The spiritual battles won't fight themselves. You can keep searching the world, but it will only fill you with regret; but if you search for the Word, it will fill you with peace—it will take you from brokenness to blessing!

Iron sharpens iron, so make sure to have godly friends in your life. Rotten fruit can destroy the whole tree.

> And take…the sword of the Spirit, which is the word of God. (Ephesians 6:17)

Stay in the Word. Sharpen yourself in the Word of God so you are prepared and wise to the lies of the enemy.

> For the word of God is alive and active. Sharper than any double-edged sword, it penetrates even to dividing soul and spirit, joints and marrow; it judges the thoughts and attitudes of the heart. (Hebrews 4:12 NIV)

David won so many battles because he gave it to God and didn't try to do it himself. If you take on a battle, you will surely fail, but if you go to God and ask for help, you will surely be victorious. The same God who was with David when he faced Goliath is with you. If there's a Goliath in front of you, that just means there's a David inside of you.

> You come against me with sword and spear and javelin, but I come against you in the name of the LORD Almighty, the God of the armies of Israel, whom you have defied. (1 Samuel 17:45 NIV)

David didn't say he came in his own power; he came with the Word of God!

Worldly Worries

I believe the Lord is speaking to you today:

> My child, I ask you to let go. Let go of
> the world and to grab onto the Word. Let
> go and trust. I ask you to believe in Me
> and not the foolish things life has to show
> you. Set your eyes on Me. Don't be con-
> formed to this world, but be transformed.
>
> Oh, My child, I call out for you to change,
> for you are set apart and not aligned with
> the rest. Let go of all these worldly wor-
> ries and change the world. I've called
> you for change—not to be changed *by* the
> world but to *change* the world.
>
> Let your heart rest, for this is not a test.
> It may feel lonely, but I am closer then
> a brother or friend. Let go of the world
> and grab My hand. Stop the worry and
> trust that I will make something beautiful

out of you. Let go of the worldly worries; they are not for you to worry about.

> And we all, who with unveiled faces contemplate the Lord's glory, are being transformed into his image with ever-increasing glory, which comes from the Lord, who is the Spirit. (2 Corinthians 3:18 NIV)

I've called you and set you apart to be different, to change this broken world. Do not stand in alignment with what is wrong, but stand up for what is right. I have given you strength when the evil one calls you weak. I've given you sound sleep when he tries to torment you. Why would you believe his lies when I've given you truth.

Don't be scared to trust Me. Don't listen to fear but listen to trust. I give you freedom when he tries to trap you, so don't listen to the world, but listen to Me. Listen to the sound of My voice, and you shall be set free. Stop the worry. Put the worry down and pick up the Word.

Truth Will Set You Free

The belt of truth holds all the other pieces of the armor together. In John 14:6, Jesus said, "I am the way, the truth, and the life. No one comes to the Father except through Me."

The truth will set you free. Lying won't get you very far, especially in the kingdom. We must denounce the lies of the enemy, the biggest liar of all, and fight back with truth from Scripture.

- When he says you are not enough, tell him, "I am more then enough because the Lord God has qualified me and said I am enough."

- When he says you are a disappointment, remind him, "Through Christ Jesus, I am not a disappointment, but a asset to the kingdom!"

- When he tries to convince you that your promise isn't coming, remind him of the covenants with Noah, Abraham, Moses, David, and the new covenant.

The enemy is the great deceiver and he wants us to rot in hell. But not even demons want to be in hell. They asked Jesus to send them into the herd of pigs instead of sending them back to hell. In Matthew 8:28-32, when Jesus came into the country of the Gergesenes, he met two violent, demon-possessed men coming out of the tombs. These two men were full of horrible demons. When Jesus cast the demons out of the men, the demons begged him to go into a heard of swine that were feeding nearby. All Jesus had to say was "go" and they were gone—and the two men were set free!

> The thief comes only to steal and kill and destroy; I have come that they may have life, and have it to the full. (John 10:10 NIV)

It only took a two-letter word to rebuke hundreds of demons. Cast down the lies of the enemy with truth! Sometimes truth will offend man, but we are not here to please man, but to please God.

Speak your truth!

Faith Over Failure

We have a very faithful God, but we must guard our faith. Put all your faith in God and watch how it will pay off. Give Him everything! It's easy to put faith in a God who hasn't failed yet.

So what is the difference between faithfulness and failure?

The word *faithful* refers to remaining loyal and steadfast while failure is a lack of success.

This world will give you failure after failure no matter what the situation: a bad doctors report, addiction, bondage, or lies from the enemy. But God wants to take that all and free you from that burden. IT'S TIME TO GET UP OUT OF THAT GRAVE! Rise up; we have a "right-now" God, which means your time is now. No more failure, but faith.

Preacher, arise; worshipper, arise; prophet, arise—you've been called, now rise up to your call!

> Now faith is the substance of things hoped for, the evidence of things not seen. (Hebrews 11:1)

Just because you can't see what God has for you, doesn't mean He has nothing for you. There is something special set apart just for you! He cares for each of us and knows us by name. He is a personal God who knows the desires of your heart. Start thanking God for the things that didn't happen because of His protection for your calling. And thank Him for the promises that haven't come to pass yet. He hasn't broken a promise yet, so it will come to pass!

> Jesus replied, "You do not realize now what I am doing, but later you will understand." (John 13:7 NIV)

You may not know how it will happen, but have faith for it because it's everything you have ever wanted and more! You may not be able to see it, but 2 Corinthians 5:7 says, "We walk by faith not by sight."

Walk in that faith—it will keep you going toward the promise. Your faith will shield you from the enemy's plans to make you fail because God's plans for you are to excel!

> Above all, taking the shield of faith with which you will be able to quench all the fiery darts of the wicked one. And take the helmet of salvation, and the sword of the Spirit, which is the word of God; praying always with all prayer and supplication in the Spirit. (Ephesians 6:16-18)

Stay alert by hanging in there and praying for all believers.

Holy Arsenal

Y ou are prepared and guarded with the whole armor
of Christ.

> Therefore take up the whole armor of
> God, that you may be able to withstand in
> the evil day, and having done all, to stand.
> Stand therefore, having girded your waist
> with truth, having put on the breastplate
> of righteousness, and having shod your
> feet with the preparation of the gospel of
> peace; above all, taking the shield of faith
> with which you will be able to quench all
> the fiery darts of the wicked one. And take
> the helmet of salvation, and the sword
> of the Spirit, which is the word of God.
> (Ephesians 6:13-17)

With this armor, you are equipped to take on those
spiritual battles, and as long as you do it with God, you
will always be victorious. You are blessed and highly
favored. As the children of God, we are the apple of His
eye. He will defend us in our time of need, be a shoulder

to cry on, and collects our tears as prayers; He sticks closer then a brother!

Always remember that there is power in prayer. No matter what situation you are going through, He will walk with you through it, and you will excel with Him by your side.

You have a holy arsenal on your side; make sure you are using it!

Part 2: Testimonies for the Kingdom

Father to the Fatherless

By Jamie Williams

I am a true example that God is a Father to the father-less. My dad passed away when I was ten years old, and to say my family and I were heartbroken is an under-statement. We all fell into a deep depression and I was hit the hardest. I was completely heartbroken because I didn't just lose my father, but my best friend as well.

As I grew farther from the Word and closer to the world I finally hit rock bottom. Every day I thought about killing myself. The enemy would taunt me, telling me lies and giving me nightmares. I didn't have sound sleep for almost three years. I avoided going to sleep so I would not have to face the nightmares. My days and nights were completely mixed up. I came to a point when I would cry every time I would have to go to bed because it was so terrifying.

There were people in my life who shouldn't of been there who were pulling me farther away from the Lord. Three years went by without me saying a prayer; without

41

opening my Bible—and without an ounce of faith that my life would change. I was in so much pain every day that it was a struggle just to get out of bed. The enemy was running free and ruining my life day by day, and I didn't even know or understand that there were blinders on my eyes.

But one day there was a reckoning. That "BUT GOD" moment happened in my life that started change and made this book possible! Little things like my phone getting taken away from me saved my life. It was such a small thing, but it was corrupting me every day. It's the little foxes that spoil the vine (Song of Solomon 2:15).

During that time, I had nothing else but my Bible and water. It was like I was in a prison, but it's the intimate time I had with the Lord that saved my life. I opened my Bible for the first time in three years; I started getting into the Word and realized that it wasn't God but the devil putting me through this pain!

Every good gift comes from God, but not every gift. Even the world has gifts wrapped in bows.

I had a dream that saved my life. In the dream, I was going to kill myself but before I did, I asked the Lord, "God, what do I have to live for?" And my four-year-old baby brother answered and said that my family and friends were all praying for me to LIVE!

But the very next day I woke up and had to kill my flesh the whole day. I had this standard in my head called "being normal," and that depression was wrong and nobody else goes through it. Well, let me tell you that you are not alone if you are suffering with depression right now. I suffered through the same pain you are facing today. When I turned to God, the heavy weight and burden of depression fell off my back and God gave me freedom! The enemy tried to kill me with the spirt of suicide hovering over my life. I truly believe it was for such a time as this; he tried to kill me for the same reason that God made me—for this book.

One day I got in the car with my mom to go to a women's meeting and I started to cry. I told my mom what I was going through and she said to me, "That's not wrong; that's your testimony." Sometimes trying to please the standards of man is the very thing that can end it all for you. That same night I gave my testimony about girls in the waiting. Little did I know that it wasn't weird because more girls and women then I could count started texting me that they had also experienced depression. I wasn't alone.

A few months later the Lord opened a door through my youth pastors, Mary and Henry Turner, and I gave my testimony at a youth meeting. Then a couple months after that I went to a revival meeting that changed my life. I felt the presence of the Lord like I have never felt it before. I screamed in my prayer language for two hours and I danced, prayed, and rejoiced!

The Lord gave me beauty for ashes, He traded my pain for promise, and turned my despair into destiny. He resurrected me; I may not have looked dead on the outside, but on the inside I was a dead man walking.

I started to see the progression all the wonderful things that happened as a result my phone getting taken away:

- After my phone was taken away, my relationship with the Lord began
- From the dream I had, my testimony came
- From that youth meeting, I started to get fresh revelation
- From that revival, this book was birthed!

No matter what you are going through, the Lord will walk with you. The Bible says that when a thief is caught, he has to pay everything back seven-fold. Here is what I was paid back:

- My joy
- My hope
- My relationship with my family
- My life
- My dreams
- My praise
- Most of all, my relationship with God!

You are Heard

By Jamie Catherine

John 1:48-50 says,

> Nathanael said to Him, "How do You
> know me?" Jesus answered and said to
> him, "Before Philip called you, when you
> were under the fig tree, I saw you." Na-
> thanael answered and said to Him, "Rab-
> bi, You are the Son of God! You are the
> King of Israel!" Jesus answered and said
> to him, "Because I said to you, 'I saw you
> under the fig tree,' do you believe? You
> will see greater things than these."

A few years ago, I was going through a hard time.
My mom and I were coming out of a broken home,
and it was hard. I was hurt, broken, I had unforgive-
ness towards my father, and I didn't feel like God was
listening to me.

Sometimes we feel like God doesn't see us and nothing is changing, but He is listening. He hears our every
thought and prayer!

> In my distress I called upon the LORD, and
> cried out to my God; He heard my voice
> from His temple, and my cry came before
> Him, *even* to His ears. (Psalm 18:6)

The Bible doesn't say that David got what he was crying out to the Lord for but he had faith that God heard him.

We don't know exactly why Nathanael was under the fig tree, but it was clearly personal between him and God. Maybe he was hurting and pouring his heart out to God and didn't feel seen. But God heard him!

Even when we feel like nobody is listening, God always hears us; He delights in hearing our every thought and prayer. No matter how you feel and how broken you are, God always wants to hear your heart.

Rescue

By Mary Davis Burns

The definition of the Word *rescue* is "To free or deliver from any confinement, violence, danger or evil; to liberate from restraint."[1] When someone is rescued, they are saved from some sort of danger, like when someone is drowning at sea, a lifesaver ring can be thrown at a person to save them from drowning.

This is what I feel like the Lord is saying to you today:

> My child, I ask you to not just read with your eyes, but read with your heart. Sometimes things are beyond what the eye can see. Things are happening that your eyes cannot focus on, and there are times when I feel your heart ache and I see your tears fall into My hands; your worries and anxiety, the hurt and fears you carry with you are weighing you down. You try to swim across the waters but you are filled with

1. Noah Webster, *Webster's Collegiate Dictionary*, s.v. "rescue," (G. & C. Merriam Co., Springfield, MA, 1913).

doubts and frustration. You get impatient and forget to pace yourself and breathe.

You ask Me, "Why, God, have You not rescued me? Why, God, do I feel this way? Why is this happening to me?" My child, this is not happening *to* you, this is happening *for* you. How can I rescue you when you won't let Me? My child, to be rescued is to "release" and be set free! Pray for strength to keep the faith and hold on during these times.

Yes, your heart is troubled, but My child, there is a time when pride must stop. The situation is out of your control and beyond your capabilities; you must stop fighting the battle and hand your sword to Me. The strength to pray is the strength to let go, release yourself, and be delivered from all that is weighing you down. Then you can grab on to the lifesaver and let Me pull you through to the other side.

Imagine that you are drowning and a life-guard comes to save you. They throw out the lifesaver ring, but does it save you without an effort on your side? You need to stop trying to stay above the water and grab onto it. You have to accept the help and be pulled in. When I come for you,

I am always near and waiting for you to accept this deliverance, the emancipation from these worldly worries. Don't you want to be free of it all and feel the relief, peace, and victory I am waiting to give you?

To learn to swim you must learn to stay afloat, taking the time and putting in the effort to stay above the water. As you learn you first feel the struggle, have the fear of being stuck under the water, but sometimes the lesson isn't about learning swim on your own, but learning turn to Me to help you get across this current so it won't not pull you under. You may feel tired and grow weak from the waves coming at you, but I am bigger then any wave, any problem, any sickness, depression, anxiety, or worry. From your heart to My ears, I have it all in My hands. All you need to do is release it from your heart and give it to Me. Accept the lifesaver and let go of the struggle.

Surrender

By Daphne Harrison

When Jamie asked me to write a page for this book, I knew instantly this is where my testimony belonged, so thank you, Jamie, for asking me. I am extremely blessed to know you!

My name is Daphne Harrison. I'm a survivor, and only because I was rescued by God. When I was fourteen years old, I was diagnosed with leukemia. I went through almost three years of treatment, lots of hospital stays, and some of the hardest days of my life. The battle sure wasn't easy, but the battle wasn't mine, it was the Lord's, and that's truly the only way I made it through! God guided me out of the deep waters, never letting go of me. And He never will!

The key to making it through situations in life is surrendering. Saying, "Lord, I'm giving this to you." Give it to Him! He will take your situation and turn it into a victory. When I look at my life, I don't see the hard situations, I see the victories God gave me out of them—and you can see that too!

I wouldn't change anything my life because God has blessed me time and time again, and I'll forever praise Him for what He has done. He's always going to be the savior; let Him save you.

Overcomers

By Elizabeth Stewart

When you are in the storm, you can't see past your problems. You may feel like a hundred years have passed and you are still in the same position. You may be thinking, "God, why is this happening to me? Why can't I be like others who are better off?" Well, I know that I am a complainer, but God has taught me that I don't want another person's testimony. God equips us all for what we can handle.

My favorite story is David and Goliath. Look what God did in that situation. A little servant boy turned into a warrior, and then he became the king of Israel! God can turn any situation around at any time. I wouldn't take back any of the heartbreak, tears, hurt, or any other thing that trials have caused, because those hard times helped me become the person I am now. It also brings a greater glory to God through my testimony.

> And they overcame him by the blood of the Lamb and by the word of their testimony, and they did not love their lives to the death. (Revelation 12:11)

We are overcomers through Him today! God is still on the throne. He is still in the small still whisper.

Continue to seek His face and pray. God will get you through it, and when it is all done and you have the victory, you will look back at it and it will seem like a blink—no big deal. Go forth into the Promised Land and live in victory; you are more then a conqueror in Jesus Christ! He will lead and guide you through any circumstance. Just put your trust and hope in Him.

I want to thank Jamie Williams for asking to write this testimony. I know it blessed me, and I pray this blesses someone.

Just a Prayer Away
By Nicole Stanley

In 2015 my brother passed away. I was so hurt and sad, but I wanted to be strong for everyone else. When I was sad, I wouldn't tell anyone else because I didn't want to them to be sad, so it would all build up. There were two people I wanted to talk to, but situations came that kept me from being able to talk to them, and that made me even more sad. It all started building up.

One thing after another was happening, and the devil was really coming at me. I felt so alone. Then a couple months later, the devil came at me through my family, making me feel like everyone was against me. My own thoughts turned very negative and I would sit in my room and cry myself to sleep and nobody would know. I had a boyfriend at that time and I would talk to him on the phone, and then hang up and cry, thinking to myself, "I'm so alone. Nobody wants to bothered. I don't have friends."

I was hurting so much, but through all that, the Lord would speak to me and tell me that I wasn't alone, that He was always there to talk. Whenever I was missing my brother, He was there to give me peace. No person could take away that pain but God, and I knew He was there. I would say, "God, I know You're here, but I want someone to actually be here to talk to," and God would say, "I'm here. You can talk to Me just like you talk to any friend. I'm here."

I would feel such a peace when the Lord would speak to me, but the devil would still come at me. Finally, I went to church one Sunday and I asked someone to pray that the devil would stop trying to steal my joy. I thank God that after that day, the devil had to flee and my joy came back! I thank God so much for being with me through it all! I used to never want to share this with anyone, but I have learned that we are overcomers through the blood of the Lamb and the word of our testimony.

This book shows how God rescues us, how He can take a dark situation and bring light. And that's exactly what the Lord has done for me; He rescued me from the schemes of the enemy who thought he had another one down, who thought he could pull me apart just like that, but my God came and pulled me out of that dark pit. He brought more light than I could imagine to a situation I didn't think any good could come from. But we know that what the enemy means for evil, my God will turn around for good!

I thank God for being there. In my darkest times He shined His light on me. He was my best friend when I thought I had no one. He can be whatever you need today: a Friend, Father, Comforter—fill in the blank for what you need Him to be today. He won't leave you or forsake you. Call out to God today and let Him shine His light on your dark situation. Whatever it may be, He's just a prayer away!

Weak Made Strong
Hughie George Wilson

Set your minds on the things that are above, not on the things that are on earth. (Colossians 3:2)

I have learned a simple but powerful thought that is a biblical truth; God likes to make strong what is weak. He will find a Moses with a stutter and turn him into a leader who will lead his people out of Egypt and become His voice. He took Peter, who was a fishermen—someone most people would never expect much from—and make him someone who could turn the world upside down. God will find a Timothy who was looked down on because of his age and encourage him to keep serving. Age doesn't determine if God will use you. God likes making the weak strong.

Where do you feel weak in your life? For me, it was my mind. The term *overthinker* would of been an understatement. To overthink is to have thoughts that go out of control, thinking of unrealistic scenarios that will never happen. Overthinking is a natural problem that leads to spiritual issues. A lack of peace is found there, and affects how we see God and who He is. It even affects how we see ourselves. Overthinking will cause you to lean on yourself rather than God. The questions of when, why, and what would cause my normal life to be filled with anxiety and worry and caused me to separate myself through overthinking.

How did I become strong? Through my relationship with God. God not only transformed my thinking, he taught me how to continually transform my thoughts too. Day by Day He renews my mind by the power of the Word, and by the authority that lies in it. I take control of a thought that will lead to a lack of peace or miss what God wants to speak to me, and I bring it to the Lord.

I became strong when I gave God every part of my life. When I allowed Him into my thoughts, He took what was weak and made it strong.

Conclusion & Call to You:
by Sarah & Alex Davis

For His name sake…

When my daughter told me she wanted to write a book called *Rescue Mission for the Kingdom*, my heart filled with joy and excitement. A knew it was a God thing. I believe this book is going to resuscitate a whole generation. This book was written on the heels of 2020 from shutdowns to lockdowns caused from the pandemic of coronavirus. During the lockdown, people suffered from extreme depression which led to many cases of suicide. The cure quickly was becoming the cause. The fact is we need each other. The first rule of recovery when you suffer from mental illness is not to isolate.

In the book of Genesis, the enemy waited until Eve was alone to deceive her. Oh, how he loves to get you alone when you're at your weakest, and attack. But God—those two words have changed me and my family's life. If you have placed your faith in Jesus as your Lord and Savior, He is also with you in those moments of weakness. It says in His Word that when you are weak, He is strong.

I once had a vision that I was carrying my cross and I struggled with it. It became too heavy to carry. I fell, and it was a hard fall. Weeping, I cried out to Jesus and said, "I'm sorry that I have failed you." He spoke to me in a loving tender way and said, "I was waiting for you to lay it down. I never intended for you to carry it alone." In that moment, He came he picked me up and carried my cross alongside me. He told me to not feel ashamed because He also fell while carrying His cross. For years I held a strong face. I wore a mask far before they were mandatory. Fooling many, including my Christian counselor who had asked if I would like to volunteer as a counselor myself. At the time, I was so held down by the spirit of heaviness that I didn't desire to live anymore. We can fool a lot of people, but we cannot fool our Lord and Savior.

The power is in the real testimony. The anointing is in authenticity. Every single thing we go through in our life is an opportunity for God's saving grace and for His glory if we allow Him to do His thing. We serve a God of restoration and redemption. I believe someone reading this is about to step into a redemption season, and this time it is personal. You are a child of God, and He takes His children's stories very seriously. When you have placed your faith in Jesus Christ, you are sealed with His Spirit.

Most every person reading this owns some form of Apple product. When you purchase an Apple product, it has a factory seal and warranty. We have a much greater seal and warranty as a child of God! You were bought with Christ blood. You have been sealed in His Spirit. Not only that, you are under warranty. A warranty is a guarantee from the maker. Why do companies offer warranties? Because their name is on the product. Listen, our trust is in Him, and He is tied to His Word and His reputation. Yes, I said for His reputation; I hope that does not offend you. The Bible says He will show up for His name sake.

> He restores my soul; He leads me in the paths of righteousness for His name's sake. (Psalms 23:3)

> For Your name's sake, O Lord, pardon my iniquity, for it is great. (Psalms 25:11)

> For You are my rock and my fortress; therefore, for Your name's sake, lead me and guide me. (Psalms 31:3)

I know we love to make everything about us, but God is not limited. Not only will He show up save you, redeem you, and restore you for your sake, but also for His name's sake and the benefit of many. But we have to make the choice to allow Him and invite Him in. Even now as you're reading this, He is standing at the door of your heart and knocking. Are you ready to get real? He has been waiting for you. You have been carrying a load you were never intended to bear on your own. Let Him in today; this is a rescue mission for the kingdom—and this time it's personal!

If you would like to receive Jesus as your personal Lord and Savior, read this prayer.

Lord Jesus, I confess I am a sinner in need of a savior. Lord, rescue me. I ask for Your forgiveness. I call out to You to come into my heart as my Lord and Savior. Lead me by Your Spirit daily and transform me to be like You. In Jesus name I pray, Amen.

About the Author

Jamie Williams is sixteen years old and lives in northern Virginia with her grandfather, mother, and little brother. She aspires to see her peers on fire for God. She is tired of the status quo and the youth living defeated, depressed, and downcast.

Jamie is on a mission—a rescue mission for the kingdom. This book is what she hopes to be the first of many projects from this trailblazer of her generation.

CPSIA information can be obtained
at www.ICGtesting.com
Printed in the USA
BVHW051545170423
662481BV00014B/524